WONDERS OF THE WORLD

# King Tut's Tomb

Don Nardo

KIDHAVEN PRESS

*An imprint of Thomson Gale, a part of The Thomson Corporation*

THOMSON GALE™

Detroit • New York • San Francisco • San Diego • New Haven, Conn.
Waterville, Maine • London • Munich

THOMSON
GALE

Picture Credits:

Cover photo: © Hulton-Deutsch Collection/CORBIS
Corel Corporation, 5, 16, 26, 28, 41
Werner Forman/Art Resource, 8
Lee Foster/Lonely Planet Images, 23
© Christel Gerstenberg/CORBIS, 11
The Griffith Institute Asmolean Museum, Oxford, 19
© Hulton-Deutsch Collection/CORBIS, 17, 31
Photos.com, 39
Scala/Art Resource, NY, 30
© Stapleton Collection/CORBIS, 20, 34
© Underwood & Underwood/CORBIS, 32
© Sandro Vannini/CORBIS, 25, 37
© Roger Wood/CORBIS, 12, 40



*For more information, contact*
KidHaven Press
27500 Drake Rd.
Farmington Hills, MI 48331-3535
Or you can visit our Internet site at http://www.gale.com



**LIBRARY OF CONGRESS CATALOGING-IN-PUBLICATION DATA**

Nardo, Don, 1947–
King Tut's tomb / by Don Nardo.
p. cm. — (Wonders of the world)
Includes bibliographical references and index.
Contents: The brief life of a boy-king—The discovery of Tut's tomb—The tomb's fabulous contents—The curse of King Tut's tomb—How did King Tut die?
ISBN 0-7377-2352-1 (hard cover : alk. paper)
1. Tutankhamen, King of Egypt—Tomb—Juvenile literature. I. Title. II. Wonders of the world (KidHaven Press)
DT87.5.N37 2004
932'.014'092—dc22 2004017024

Printed in the United States of America

# CONTENTS

CHAPTER **ONE**

# The Brief Life of a Boy-King

Today, almost everyone has heard of King Tut. (His full name was Tutankhamun. But that is such a mouthful that it has become customary to call him Tut for short.) In fact, he has become by far the most famous of all the **pharaohs** (kings) of ancient Egypt. This is mainly because of the discovery of his tomb in 1922. It was one of the greatest moments in the history of **archaeology**, the science of digging up past cultures.

Many ancient Egyptian tombs had been found before this. But all of them had long ago been robbed of their contents. In contrast, King Tut's tomb was nearly intact. It contained hundreds of beautifully preserved objects that had been placed in it shortly after Tut's death more than three thousand years ago. Tut's **mummy** was also in the tomb. It lay inside a coffin made of three hundred pounds of solid gold.

News of the discovery quickly spread around the world. King Tut and his fabulous tomb captured the imagination of people of all walks of life in every country. And this fascination for the long-dead Egyptian ruler remains just as strong today. King Tut mania is so huge, in fact, that the Egyptian government recently had to close the tomb. More than three thousand people

Made of gold, this image of King Tut shows him holding the crook and flail, symbols of royal power.

came to tour it each day, and the dust and germs they brought inside were causing it to crumble.

## The Eighteenth Dynasty and Akhenaten

Perhaps the most remarkable thing about King Tut is the veil of mystery that surrounds him. Scholars have been diligently studying him and his burial goods for more than eight decades. Yet extremely little is known about him. The exact identity of his parents is still debated. He reached the Egyptian throne under very odd circumstances, and few of the events of his brief reign are known. Moreover, the manner of his untimely death, at about age seventeen, is also a mystery. Finally, following his death his successors tried to erase all evidence of his and his whole family's existence.

Many **Egyptologists**—experts on ancient Egypt—have tried to explain these mysteries. They begin by looking at Egypt and its royal court in the years leading up to Tut's reign. He lived in a period of Egyptian history that scholars call the New Kingdom. It began in about 1550 B.C., roughly 3,550 years ago. Before this, a group of foreign soldiers had occupied Egypt, much to the dismay of the local inhabitants. Then a strong young pharaoh named Ahmose drove out the intruders. He established a new **dynasty**, or family line of rulers—the glorious Eighteenth Dynasty. One after another, its rulers launched conquests and gained Egypt a large and powerful empire.

However, the tenth pharaoh in the line, Amenhotep IV, was very different than his predecessors. He was a

thinker and dreamer rather than a soldier. The Egyptians had long worshipped a large number of gods. But Amenhotep came to believe that there was only one god —Aten—whose face was the sun's blindingly bright disk. The pharaoh abandoned all the former gods and introduced a new religion based on worship of Aten. Amenhotep changed his name to Akhenaten, meaning

This is a stone likeness of Akhenaten (Amenhotep IV), who may have been Tut's father.

"servant of Aten." And he left the traditional Egyptian capital of Memphis and built a new capital—Akhetaten ("horizon of Aten").

## The Question of Tut's Identity

It was in the palace of this brand-new royal city that the future King Tut was born in about the year 1344 B.C. And this is where the first of the mysteries surrounding

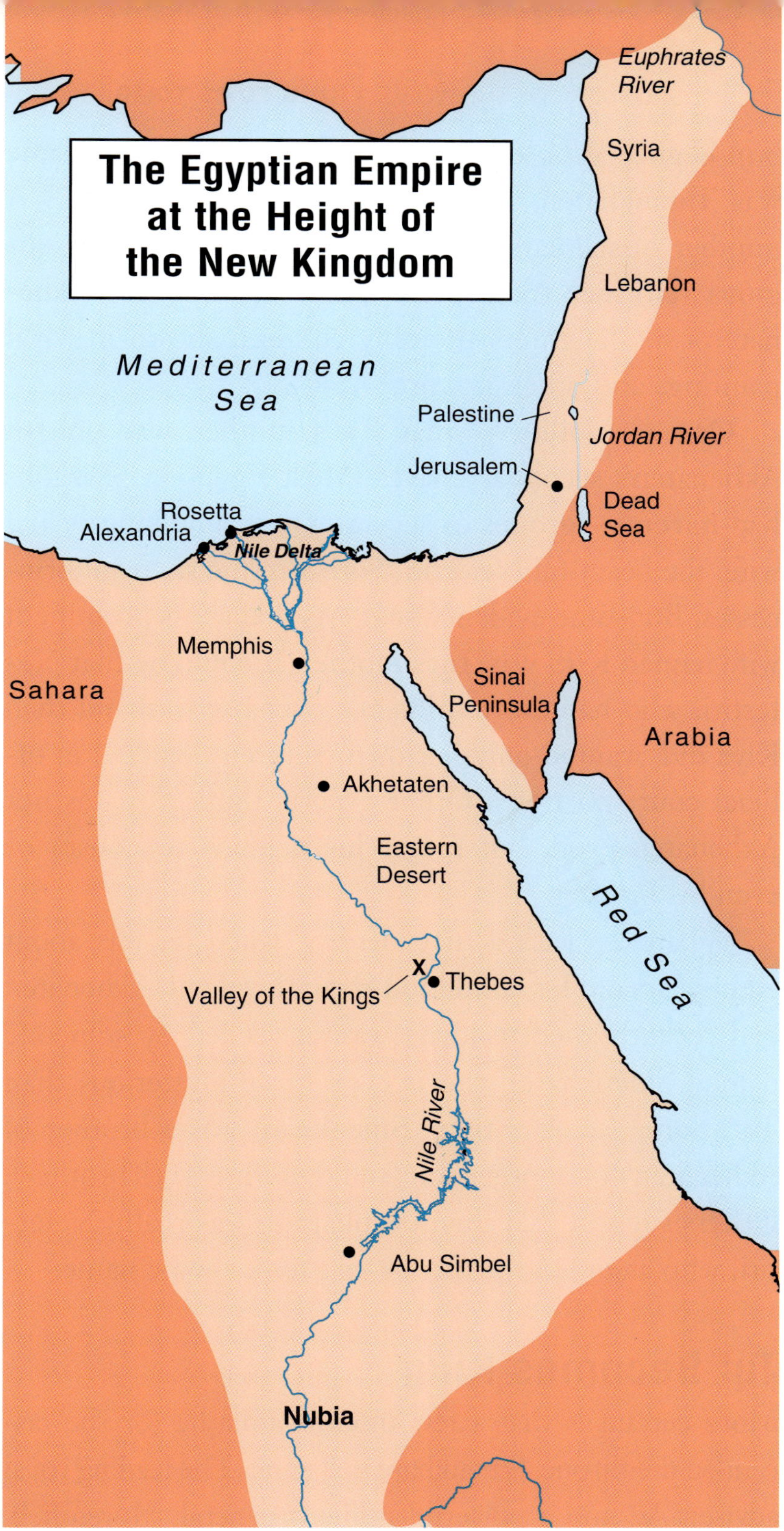
The Egyptian Empire at the Height of the New Kingdom
Euphrates River
Syria
Lebanon
Mediterranean Sea
Palestine
Jordan River
Jerusalem
Dead Sea
Rosetta
Alexandria
Nile Delta
Memphis
Sahara
Sinai Peninsula
Arabia
Akhetaten
Eastern Desert
Red Sea
X
Valley of the Kings
Thebes
Nile River
Abu Simbel
Nubia

him begins. Who exactly was this boy? His birth name was Tutankhaten, meaning "living image of Aten." A number of scholars believe he was the son of the religious reformer Akhenaten. But if so, why are Akhenaten's six daughters the only children shown in royal paintings and other artwork?

One possibility is that Tut's mother was one of Akhenaten's secondary wives. Most Egyptian pharaohs had **harems**—groups of several wives. The king's chief wife, the beautiful Nefertiti, bore him the six royal princesses. But some evidence suggests that a less prominent wife named Kiya was Tut's mother. It could be that Nefertiti, who had more influence over her husband than Kiya did, wanted only her own children depicted in official court portraits. Other experts think Tut was not Akhenaten's son, but rather his nephew or cousin or even his brother.

Whatever Tut's actual identity, when he was about eight years old his childhood abruptly ended. Akhenaten had recently died. And he was succeeded by someone named Smenkhare, who is even more mysterious than Tut. Some scholars think Smenkhare was a brother of Akhenaten's or another son (and therefore Tut's brother). Others suggest that the new pharaoh was really Nefertiti, who assumed the throne and took a male name.

## Tut Becomes King

More certain is that a few months after he (or she) ascended the throne, Smenkhare was gone. The leading royal adviser, Ay, and a powerful military general, Horemheb, took the young Tut to Memphis, where he was crowned king. Under their influence, the new pharaoh restored the old gods, including the widely revered creator-god Amun. The Egyptians were lovers of tradition. Most of them missed the old religion and had come to hate

Akhenaten's wife Nefertiti, seen here in an ancient wall painting, was probably not Tut's mother.

This wooden head of King Tut as a young child was found in his tomb.

Akhenaten and his new faith. The words carved on a surviving **stele** (slab of stone) give a good idea of the situation:

> The temples and estates of the gods and goddesses . . . had fallen into ruin. Their shrines had fallen down, turned into piles of rubble and overgrown with weeds. . . . The world was in chaos and the gods had turned their backs on this land. . . . Now [that] the gods and goddesses of this land [have been restored, they] are rejoicing in their hearts.[1]

To emphasize the dramatic change, the boy-king changed his name from Tutankhaten to Tutankhamun ("living image of Amun"). He also moved away from the city Akhenaten had created and never returned. In addition, Tut married one of Akhenaten's daughters, Ankhesenamun.

Poor Ankhesenamun soon found herself a widow, however. After a reign of only nine years, Tut died. Ay saw to it that the boy-king was **embalmed** and placed in a tomb. But the ceremony was rushed and done in secret. Why? Could it be that Ay, who now took the throne, wanted Tut out of the way and had him killed?

Four years later, Ay himself was dead, and Horemheb was the new pharaoh. Horemheb ordered the names of Akhenaten, Nefertiti, Smenkhare, Tutankhamun, and Ay to be chiseled off all monuments. He even forbade people from speaking their names. What terrible things was Horemheb trying to cover up?

The strange circumstances surrounding Tut and those he knew were eventually forgotten, just as his tomb was buried by drifting sands and forgotten. Thousands of years passed before that tomb saw the light of day again. When it did, a world the boy-king could never have imagined was eager to see its fantastic contents and to begin to solve the mysteries it concealed.

CHAPTER TWO

# The Discovery of Tut's Tomb

When the pharaoh Horemheb and his successors erased King Tutankhamun's name from the Egyptian monuments, they tried to be thorough. Before Horemheb's time, Egyptian priests had carved the names of all the pharaohs on the walls of temples. Modern scholars call these "**king-lists**." Horemheb's henchmen chiseled Tut's name off the king-lists, so for a long time modern scholars knew nothing about the boy-king and his reign.

However, those who sought to destroy all evidence that Tut had existed were not quite thorough enough. Here and there—in individual homes, tombs, and other places—some evidence for Tut remained and survived into modern times. In 1837, an Egyptologist found a piece of this evidence. It consisted of Tut's name carved onto the base of a statue. Other such tidbits came to light in the years that followed. One of the most exciting was a beautiful blue cup inscribed with Tut's name, discovered in 1906.

The place where the cup was found was of particular importance. It lay in the **Valley of the Kings**. This is the modern name for a remote area on the west bank of

Tombs like these, in the Valley of the Kings, contained objects that led to the discovery of King Tut's tomb.

Howard Carter (with the cane) walks with Egyptian workers carrying objects from Tut's tomb.

the Nile River, near the ancient Egyptian city of Thebes. The area was used as a **necropolis**, or burial ground, by many of the pharaohs of the New Kingdom.

The discovery of the cup bearing Tut's name in the Valley of the Kings led some scholars to believe that his tomb might be somewhere in that area. One of these experts was Howard Carter, an English archaeologist. He became convinced that Tut's tomb lay in some forgotten corner of the great necropolis. And he set his sights on finding the tomb, a goal he would eventually attain with spectacular results.

## New Evidence for King Tut

The blue cup was not the only clue to the existence of Tut's tomb. In January 1907, less than a year after the cup's discovery, two more finds in the Valley of the Kings excited the interest of Carter and other **excavators** (diggers). One was a small grave (now called the "Cache Tomb") containing some old jars and assorted debris. Tut's name was inscribed on the jars.

The other find was a tomb that excavators dubbed "Tomb 55." Tut's name was found in several places inside. This and other evidence suggested that the tomb had been sealed during his reign.

Carter was excited by these finds. So was his friend, George E.S.M. Hebert, Earl of Carnarvon, an English aristocrat and amateur archaeologist. Carnarvon, who had chronic health problems, had recently come to Egypt to take advantage of its dry climate, as well as to look for ancient **artifacts**. Carter told Carnarvon that Tut's tomb must lie somewhere near the Cache Tomb and Tomb 55.

## Obstacles to Overcome

Carter, a brilliant researcher, soon used these previous finds to help pinpoint a likely location for Tut's tomb. It was an unexplored patch of dirt lying near the tomb of the pharaoh Rameses VI. Carter and Carnarvon desperately wanted to dig on the spot. But it took until 1913

Lord Carnarvon takes a break from the search for Tut's tomb in the Valley of the Kings.

(about six years) to obtain permission from the Egyptian government.

To the men's frustration, just when they planned to start digging they encountered another obstacle. World War I broke out in Europe. Both men got involved in the war effort, and it was not until 1917 that they began digging in the Valley of the Kings.

As the months rolled by, the pit they dug grew deeper and deeper, and all they found was dirt, rocks, and still more dirt. Finally, in 1919, they uncovered the remains of some small huts. It turned out to be the settlement that had housed the workers who had decorated the nearby tomb of Rameses VI. Because the discovery had no connection to King Tut, Carnarvon was sorely disappointed. But Carter was convinced that they were

Howard Carter (holding the shovel) tears down a brick wall leading to a hidden section of Tut's tomb.

on the right track. If only they dug deeper, he said, they would find what they were looking for.

## "Wonderful Things"

Carter was right. The digging continued, and on November 3, 1922, the top of a stone staircase was uncovered. The removal of more dirt revealed a set of sixteen steps leading downward to a door made of mud bricks. The excavators broke through the door, revealing a rubble-strewn passageway that led to a second door.

The great moment came on November 26. Carrying a pick and some candles and accompanied by Carnarvon and Lady Carnarvon, Carter approached the second door. He later recalled:

> With trembling hands I made a tiny breach in the upper left hand corner [of the door]. . . . Then, widening the hole a little, I inserted the candle and peered in. . . . At first I could see nothing. . . . But presently, as my eyes grew accustomed to the light, details of the room emerged slowly from the mist, strange animals, statues, and gold—everywhere the glint of gold. . . . I was struck dumb with amazement, and when Lord Carnarvon . . . inquired anxiously, "Can you see anything?", it was all I could do to get out the words, "Yes, wonderful things!"[2]

For Carter, it was the discovery of a lifetime. For Tut, it was the chance to outshine those who had tried to erase the memory of his existence. After some thirty-three centuries of obscurity, the boy-king was about to become one of the most famous of all historical figures.

CHAPTER THREE

# The Tomb's Fabulous Contents

To some extent, Howard Carter was surprised at the treasure trove of artifacts he found upon entering King Tut's tomb. Earlier, on finding the outer door at the bottom of the staircase, he had noticed something that had made his heart sink. The seal on the door had been broken and then replaced in ancient times. This was a telltale sign that thieves had entered, after which palace authorities had resealed the tomb. Indeed, this turned out to be the case. Inspection of the tomb showed that robbers had broken in twice, probably not long after the boy-king was laid to rest.

Fortunately for Carter and posterity, someone or something had scared the thieves away before they had stolen very much. After the tomb had been resealed a second time, debris hid its entrance, and thereafter it was forgotten. Consequently, a majority of the objects placed inside during Tut's funeral remained there during his centuries-long sleep.

The great mass of valuable artifacts in the tomb gave people an idea of the splendor in which Egyptian pharaohs were buried. Tut was a minor king who had ruled only a few years and accomplished relatively little. And his burial had been unusually hasty and carried out in secret.

This exhibit in an Egyptian museum shows replicas of the artifacts exactly as they were found in Tut's tomb.

Considering what was found in his tomb, scholars reasoned that the finery that had originally adorned the tombs of the major pharaohs must have been truly astounding.

## A Love of Sports and Music

The artifacts in the tomb were also important for what they revealed about King Tut himself. Before Carter and Carnarvon uncovered the grave site, virtually nothing of a personal nature was known about the boy-king. What did he look like? How was his health? What activities did he enjoy? None of these questions could be answered because no descriptions of him had been found.

Various objects in the tomb helped to answer such questions. For example, several wooden writing palettes were found. They were unused, and some evidence suggests they originally belonged to one or two of Tut's half-sisters (Akhenaten's daughters). A number of scholars interpret this as proof that the boy-king was not much interested in academic pursuits. In stark contrast, the tomb was filled with hunting and sports equipment. Included were 46 bows, 427 arrows, 2 bronze swords, 2 gold daggers, 8 shields, 2 slings (for hunting birds and other small game), and 6 full-sized chariots. Clearly, the boy-king was an avid hunter who loved outdoor activities.

Other artifacts found in the tomb show that Tut greatly enjoyed music. There were several musical instruments. Among these was a **sistrum**, a device with handles topped with a series of small metal disks. It made a rattling noise when shaken. Nearby, a small

This dagger with a golden handle and sheath is one of the many weapons found in Tut's tomb.

wooden shrine bore a painting of Tut's wife, Ankhesenamun, playing such an instrument while he watched.

## The Coffins and Mummy

The painting on the shrine was not the only visual representation of Tut in the tomb. Several wooden figurines, wrapped in linen shawls, appeared to depict him. Also, the king's coffins were carved and painted with faces that probably bear a strong resemblance to his. There were three coffins, which Carter found nested within one another. The outer two were made of wood and the third of pure gold.

Inside the innermost coffin, the excavators found Tut's mummy, which had been undisturbed by the tomb

Ancient Egyptian artisans made this golden image of Tut on the third and innermost coffin.

robbers. The face was covered by a magnificent gold mask. This mask was decorated with precious stones, including quartz, lapis lazuli, and turquoise. The boy-king's arms were crossed, and his hands held the crook and flail, traditional symbols wielded by Egyptian kings.

(The crook, shaped like a hook, represented the government. The flail, which looks like a small mop on the end of a stick, represented the gods.)

Examination of the body revealed that Tut was about five feet six inches tall in life. He was beardless and had pierced ears. Unfortunately, the corpse had decayed so much that it was impossible to tell his hair color. Carter was not surprised to find the internal organs missing. It was the custom to remove these and place them in special containers. The excavators found the remains of Tut's organs inside a small shrine situated a few feet from the coffins.

## A Well-Stocked Afterlife

Though impressive, the sporting equipment, weapons, figurines, coffins, mummy, and shrines comprised only a small portion of the total contents of the tomb. There was also a great deal of furniture. Carter and his assistants counted six chairs, twelve stools, six beds, and sixty-nine storage chests and boxes. One of the chairs is a splendid thronelike piece decorated in gold, with a stunning painted carving on the back showing Tut and his young wife in their throne room.

Following ancient Egyptian beliefs, the furniture was intended for Tut's use in the afterlife. So were numerous other items placed in the tomb. There were many pieces of clothing, including kilts, tunics, shirts, caps, and gloves. And to nourish the king in the afterlife, the tomb was stocked with food and drink. The excavators found containers of bread, beef, poultry, spices, fruits, nuts,

Found on the back of King Tut's throne, this carving shows Tut and his young bride in their royal court.

and honey. There were also several jars of wine. (No wine was left in them. Experts calculate that all of the wine evaporated through the porous pottery in the space of only three years.)

One of the most unexpected, and saddest, finds in the tomb was that of two mummified infants. Were these the stillborn children of Tut and Ankhesenamun? Carter and his colleagues had no way of knowing. Here was one more mystery to add to the many unsolved ones surrounding the young man in the golden coffin.

CHAPTER FOUR

# The Curse of King Tut's Tomb

Some of the mysteries surrounding King Tut and his tomb revolved around such matters as his identity and the manner of his death. These helped to fuel the Tut mania that swept the world in the months following the discovery of the tomb. Howard Carter described the commotion in a letter to a friend:

> The [local] telegraph office was completely buried under a deluge [flood] of newspaper dispatches. Tourist shops quickly sold out their stocks of camera and film. . . . The two leading hotels [in the nearby town] set up tents in their gardens where many guests were fortunate to be accommodated for a single night on army cots.[3]

However, the tomb-related mystery that gripped the public more than any other was the one involving the so-called curse of King Tut's tomb. In the months and years following the opening of the tomb, a number of strange occurrences were reported in newspapers. These included the deaths of some of those who had entered the tomb. Some people attributed these eerie happenings to a curse that had been placed on the tomb in ancient times. Others said that no such curse existed. A heated debate erupted, one that continues to this day. Was the curse real and something that people should be frightened of? Or was it superstition and not to be taken seriously?

Tut's coffin can be seen beneath a colorful wall painting in this photo of the king's burial chamber.

Some people worried that Howard Carter (left) had unleashed an ancient curse by opening Tut's tomb.

## A Chilling Series of Events

Those who argue that the curse was real point to the chilling series of events that took place in the months directly after the discovery of Tut's tomb in November 1922. Early in 1923, the *New York Times* printed a letter sent by Maria Corelli. She was a noted American writer of horror tales. She claimed that she owned an old book written in ancient Arabic. Corelli said that a passage in the book warned that any persons who entered a pharaoh's tomb would be struck dead. Therefore, dire consequences might ensue for Carter, Carnarvon, and others who had violated King Tut's tomb.

Sure enough, at about 2:00 A.M. on April 5, 1923, only a few weeks after Corelli issued her warning, Lord Carnarvon died. At that same moment, one newspaper said, all of the lights in Cairo (Egypt's capital) went out. Not long afterward, an English newspaper reported another spooky incident. Back in England, Carnarvon's dog, Susie, had howled loudly and dropped dead at 2:00 A.M., the same time her master had met his doom.

Carter carries artifacts from the tomb. He was convinced that the curse was nonsense.

A few days after these disquieting events, a newspaper reporter interviewed the famous writer Sir Arthur Conan Doyle. Doyle had invented the master detective Sherlock Holmes. The reporter asked Doyle what he thought about the recent events in Egypt. Doyle replied that he thought there might be a curse on King Tut's tomb. His remarks were picked up by other news outlets, and the curse became a worldwide sensation.

Soon, other information of an ominous nature was revealed. Another newspaper reported that Carter and Carnarvon had found the curse spelled out in ancient Egyptian characters on the tomb's door. It read: "They who enter this sacred tomb shall swift be visited by wings of death."[4] This seemed to confirm that the excavators had been duly warned that they should stay clear of the tomb.

## False and Misleading Statements?

Those who believed the curse was nonsense responded to these supposedly weird episodes in the following manner. First, Lord Carnarvon was a sick and frail man long before the tomb was found. He was bitten by a mosquito early in 1923 and developed an infection. Partly because antibiotics did not yet exist, he grew weaker and died, not unusual under the circumstances. Moreover, the critics pointed out, close investigation revealed that only the lights in Cairo's hospital, not the entire city, had gone out. And such power failures were common at the time.

In addition, the critics said, investigators could not confirm the death of Carnarvon's dog, Susie. In any case, the claim that they died at the same time did not hold up. Carnarvon was in Egypt and Susie in England. These places are in different time zones, so 2:00 A.M. in England is not the same time as 2:00 A.M. in Egypt.

Even more telling was the fact that no curse was written on the tomb's door, as mistakenly reported in the press. Furthermore, Carnarvon was the only major figure who had entered the tomb who died shortly after-

Lord Carnarvon, his wife, and Howard Carter stand outside Tut's tomb. Carnarvon died shortly after this photo was taken.

ward. One would think that Carter, who found the tomb and worked in it almost every day for ten years, would be marked for death. But he lived another seventeen years. Lady Evelyn, Carnarvon's daughter, was one of the first people who set foot in the tomb. But she survived until 1980, dying at age seventy-nine. And Dr. D.E. Derry, who performed a physical exam on Tut's body, lived until 1969.

Thus, the critics say, the so-called evidence for the curse was a collection of false and misleading statements. Those who believe in the curse remain unconvinced, however. They insist that opening King Tut's tomb released dark, ancient forces into the modern world. One thing is certain. Arguments over the curse are likely to keep Tut mania alive and well for generations to come.

CHAPTER
FIVE

# How Did King Tut Die?

Outside of the famous curse of King Tut's tomb, the most hotly debated mystery surrounding the boy-king is the manner of his death. Was he murdered? Did he die in an accident? Or was his untimely end the result of natural causes? In trying to answer these questions, archaeologists, doctors, and other experts have closely examined Tut's mummy. Their findings have yet to resolve the cause of his death. But they have suggested some interesting possibilities for his demise. They have also shed some fascinating light on the riddle of who Tut was.

## Examinations of the Mummy

The question of Tut's death was on the minds of Howard Carter and other experts from the moment they entered the tomb and found the boy-king's remains. After all, Tut died in his teens. At an age when most young men are strong, vigorous, and full of life, the boy-king had met his end. There had to be some noteworthy cause.

The first step taken to solve this mystery was an autopsy (physical exam of a corpse). It was performed by Dr. D.E. Derry shortly after the opening of the tomb. His physical exam turned up no obvious causes for the boy-king's death. X-rays might have determined the cause, but Dr. Derry was unable to X-ray the body at the time.

More than forty years passed before the Egyptian government gave permission for an X-ray exam of Tut's mummy. The exam took place in 1968 under the supervision of R.G. Harrison of England's Liverpool University. Harrison found a spot

A ceremonial shield found in the tomb shows King Tut killing a lion.

behind the body's left ear where the skull bone was abnormally thin. He said that it was likely caused by pressure resulting from bleeding inside the brain. This might have been caused by a blow to the back of the head, Harrison suggested.

Based on this evidence, in the years that followed a number of scholars and writers proposed that King Tut had been murdered. The most likely suspects in these accounts were the boy-king's successors—Ay and Horemheb. Both men obviously benefited from Tut's untimely passing.

## A Hunting Accident?

However, many scholars remain unconvinced that Tut was murdered. First, they point out that it is highly unlikely a murderer armed with a blunt instrument would strike someone behind the left ear. Such blows usually come down on the top of the head.

Also, say critics of the murder theory, the thin skull bone and bleeding beneath it could have had other causes. Tut could have fallen and accidentally struck his head, for instance. The piles of weapons and sporting gear found in the tomb show that he was an avid hunter, and it was not unusual for ancient hunters to fall from their chariots. On the other hand, the pressure on Tut's skull could have been caused by natural causes, including some kind of tumor.

## Two Mummies Compared

The physical exams of Tut's body also generated some clues to his identity. Was he Akhenaten's son, as some

An ancient wall painting shows the pharaoh Horemheb (center). Some experts believe he was involved in Tut's death.

scholars had long held? First, Harrison's X-ray exam established that the boy-king's skull was oddly shaped. It was flatter than normal on top and longer than normal in the back. Also, Tut's arms had some unusual abnormalities near the joints.

A number of scholars have compared these findings to those of an X-ray exam of a mummy found in Tomb 55. (This is the tomb that appeared to have been sealed while Tut was king.) Both Tut and the person buried in Tomb 55 had the same odd features of the head and arms. The results of blood tests performed on the two mummies were also revealing. Both had identical blood types. This seems to confirm that Tut was closely related to the person in the other tomb.

This statue shows Tut hunting. Some scholars suggest that Tut died as the result of a hunting accident.

In this painting, Ay (right), one of the murder suspects, performs a traditional funeral ceremony for Tut.

Based on these studies, some experts think that the mummy in Tomb 55 is that of Tut's mysterious successor, Smenkhare. That would make the two men brothers or perhaps close cousins. Others argue that the body in Tomb 55 is that of Akhenaten, proving that the pharoah was indeed Tut's father.

## Why Was the Burial Rushed?

None of these theories based on exams of Tut's body directly addresses another riddle about him—one posed by the contents of his tomb. Why was his burial so rushed and held in secret? Could that have some bearing on the question of whether he was murdered? Some writers have suggested that Ay killed Tut to gain the throne. And the new king hastily and secretly buried the old one in order to cover up the crime.

Another, more likely theory has recently been put forward by some scholars. They suggest that Tut died rather suddenly, either in an accident or by natural causes. Both Ay and Horemheb had designs on the throne. But at the time of the boy-king's death, Horemheb was away on a military campaign. According to this scenario, Ay tried to keep news of the king's death from Horemheb as long as possible. That way Ay could grab the throne before the general had a chance to return to the capital and challenge him.

There is no way to know if this actually happened. After all, Tut, Ay, Horemheb, Smenkhare, and the others took their secrets with them to their graves. It is possible that most of the riddles surrounding Tut and his tomb will never be solved. Yet people are sure to keep trying to solve them, for the deepest mysteries are always the ones that excite the human imagination the most.

# Notes

## Chapter One: The Brief Life of a Boy-King

1. Quoted in Christine El Mahdy, *Tutankhamen: The Life and Death of the Boy-King*. New York: St. Martin's, 1999, pp. 317–19.

## Chapter Two: The Discovery of Tut's Tomb

2. Howard Carter, *The Tomb of Tutankhamen.* London: Dover, 1985 (reprint of the 1923 edition), pp. 95–96.

## Chapter Four: The Curse of King Tut's Tomb

3. Quoted in El Mahdy, *Tutankhamen*, pp. 68–69.

4. Quoted in Tutankhamun's Curse, http://homepage.powerup.com.au/~ancient/curse.htm.

# Glossary

**archaeology:** The science of digging up and studying past cultures.

**artifacts:** Old objects belonging to past cultures.

**autopsy:** Medical examination of a dead body.

**dynasty:** A line of rulers belonging to a single family.

**Egyptologist:** A scholar who specializes in ancient Egypt.

**embalm:** To preserve a dead body prior to burial.

**excavator:** Someone who digs in the ground.

**harem:** A group of wives who are all married to one male ruler.

**king-list:** A list of kings written or carved on old walls or monuments.

**mummy:** The remains of a dead person who has been embalmed and wrapped in strips of cloth.

**necropolis:** A burial ground or cemetery.

**pharaoh:** A king of ancient Egypt.

***sistrum:*** An ancient musical instrument that made a rattling sound.

**stele:** A slab of stone or wood on which ancient people wrote or carved names and messages.

**Valley of the Kings:** A remote, rocky area on the west bank of the Nile River where many pharaohs of the New Kingdom created their tombs.

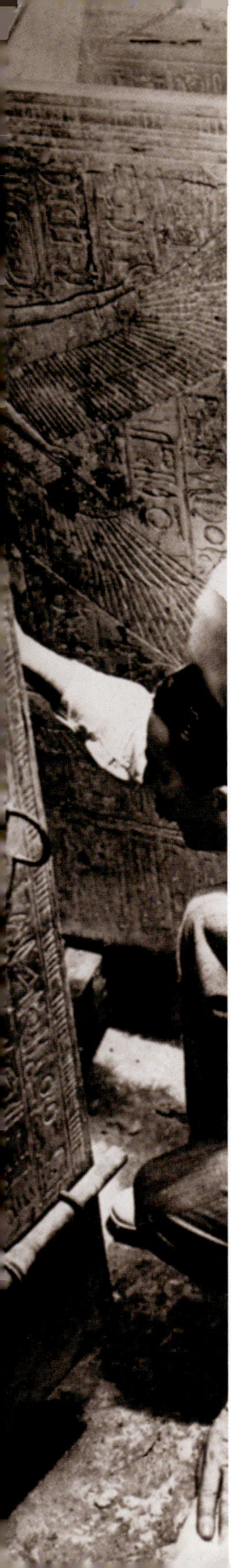

# For Further Exploration

## Books

Michael R. King et al., *Who Killed King Tut?* Amherst, NY: Prometheus, 2004. A well-written volume in which modern forensic experts attempt to piece together the surviving clues to Tut's demise.

Anne Millard, *Mysteries of the Pyramids.* Brookfield, CT: Copper Beech Books, 1995. Aimed at basic readers, this book by a noted scholar is short but brightly illustrated and filled with interesting facts about the pyramids and ancient Eqyptian life.

Neil Morris, *Atlas of Ancient Egypt.* New York: NTC Contemporary Publishing, 2000. This excellent book about ancient Eqypt contains many maps and also several impressive double-page spreads of specific eras and aspects of everyday life.

David Murdock, *Tutankhamun: The Life and Death of a Pharaoh.* London: Dorling Kindersley, 1998. A beautifully illustrated examination of an Egyptian ruler who died young and was later forgotten, only to become famous in modern times when scholars unearthed his tomb.

Kelly Trumble, *Cat Mummies.* Boston: Houghton Mifflin, 1999. An unusual and nicely illustrated volume that tells why cats were important in ancient Egyptian society and how these animals were mummified.

## Web Sites

**Curse of King Tut's Tomb** (www.mummytombs.com/eqypt/kingtut.htm) Tells how the curse came about and the many claimed effects it had on people connected with the excavation of Tut's tomb.

**The King Tut Investigation** (www.iois.net/Tutinvestigation.htm). An overview of the Discovery Channel documentary exploring the possibility that Tut was murdered.

**Tutankhamun** (http://homepage.powerup.com.au/~ancient/tut1.htm). A useful overview of King Tut and his tomb, with color photos and links to related topics.

# Index

# About the Author

Historian and award-winning writer Don Nardo has written or edited numerous books about the ancient world. Among these are *Life in Ancient Athens*, *Greek and Roman Sport*, *Egyptian Mythology*, *Empires of Mesopotamia*, and the *Greenhaven Encyclopedia of Greek and Roman Mythology*. He lives with his wife, Christine, in Massachusetts.